HOW IT WORKS

THE INTERNET

by Angie Smibert

FOCUS READERS

FOCUS READERS

WWW.FOCUSREADERS.COM

Focus Readers is distributed by North Star Editions:
sales@northstareditions.com | 888-417-0195

Produced for Focus Readers by Red Line Editorial.

Content Consultant: Diane Pozefsky, Research Professor and Director of Undergraduate Studies, Department of Computer Science, University of North Carolina at Chapel Hill

Photographs ©: Uber Images/Shutterstock Images, cover, 1; Andrey Popov/iStockphoto, 4–5; Marco Piunti/iStockphoto, 6; AP Images, 8; Maximumm/Shutterstock Images, 10–11; ivan_m/iStockphoto, 13; dotshock/Shutterstock Images, 14; Red Line Editorial, 15; nmedia/Shutterstock Images, 16–17; FatCamera/iStockphoto, 19; Mutlu Kurtbas/iStockphoto, 20; iinspiration/Shutterstock Images, 23; Yalana/iStockphoto, 24–25; mikkelwilliam/iStockphoto, 26; Askold Romanov/iStockphoto, 29

ISBN
978-1-63517-235-5 (hardcover)
978-1-63517-300-0 (paperback)
978-1-63517-430-4 (ebook pdf)
978-1-63517-365-9 (hosted ebook)

Library of Congress Control Number: 2017935880

Printed in the United States of America
Mankato, MN
June, 2017

ABOUT THE AUTHOR

Angie Smibert is the author of several young adult novels, including the Memento Nora series, dozens of short stories, and numerous educational titles about science and technology. She was also a writer and online training developer at NASA's Kennedy Space Center for many years. She received NASA's prestigious Silver Snoopy as well as several other awards for her work.

TABLE OF CONTENTS

People
Search
My Status
My Page
My Friends
My Photos
My Videos
My Groups
Apps
Pages
Interests

CHAPTER 1

WHAT IS THE INTERNET?

Long ago, if people wanted to communicate, they wrote letters. News took days or even months to get from place to place. Today, people can share photos or send e-mail with just a tap on a screen. They can also video chat with friends or stream movies. The Internet makes all of this possible.

Many people use social networks to connect with friends on the Internet.

Sending e-mail is a popular use for the Internet.

The Internet is a network of networks. It allows computers to share tasks and send information. Today, the Internet has billions of users. But it began as a small network of only two computers.

The network was called ARPAnet. It was created in the autumn of 1969. Researchers used it to send messages between two universities in California.

At first, ARPAnet connected only these two computers. By December 1969, the network had four computers. ARPAnet continued to grow throughout the 1970s and 1980s. Other organizations began their own networks, too.

All these different networks connected to each other. A computer that was part of one network could share information with computers on any of the other networks. Together, these networks came to be known as the Internet.

At first, only universities, government agencies, and nonprofit organizations could use the Internet. Most people did not know it existed.

Netscape was one of the first web browsers.

That began to change in the 1990s. In 1991, Tim Berners-Lee introduced the **World Wide Web**. The Web was a new way to get information on the Internet. The Web uses **hypertext**. Hypertext can link documents together. Users can click on text or graphics. This takes them to a different **web page**. Hypertext made websites and search engines possible. People began using **web browsers** to view websites. New rules also allowed people to start using the Internet to buy and sell things in 1991.

Because of these changes, many more people could use the Internet. By 1992, the Internet had approximately 7,500 networks. It connected more than 1 million computers.

CRITICAL THINKING

How has the Internet changed the way people communicate with one another?

MASTER
ONLINE
OFFLINE
RE0
RE1
FAN
PEM
ACO/LT
YELLOW ALARM
RED ALARM
OK
FAIL
SATA SSD 1
SATA SSD 2

CHAPTER 2

WIRES, CABLES, AND RADIO WAVES

The Internet allows people to send files from one device to another. Sending a file involves several steps. First, the device must connect to the Internet. A cable or phone line connects the device to an Internet service provider (ISP). An ISP is a company that sells access to the Internet.

Information is sent along the Internet through cables and wires.

Each ISP has its own network. To reach other networks, the ISP connects to a large switching facility called an Internet exchange point (IXP). Smaller ISPs often connect to other ISPs. Larger ISPs connect to the backbones of the Internet. An Internet backbone is a network made up of high-speed and high-capacity lines. Backbones are like major highways for information. They carry an enormous amount of traffic.

As information travels along an Internet backbone, it might pass through **servers** and other devices on each network. These devices help the information reach the correct destination.

Many devices use an Ethernet cable to connect to the Internet.

Every device on the Internet has a unique number. This number is called an Internet **protocol** (IP) address. IP addresses are long strings of numbers. They can be hard to remember. So IP addresses are often matched up with domain names. A domain name is made up of letters. It is part of a uniform resource locator (URL), or website address.

Servers are often grouped together in server rooms, also known as server farms.

When a person types a domain name, a request goes to a local domain name server (DNS). The DNS looks up the IP address that matches the domain name. If the DNS does not know the IP address that matches the domain name, it can send requests to other servers to find the address. Then the DNS connects the person's computer to that address.

A **router** is a special kind of server. Routers direct the flow of information. They send each file toward its destination. They can even send files across oceans. Undersea cables connect hubs on each continent.

PARTS OF A URL

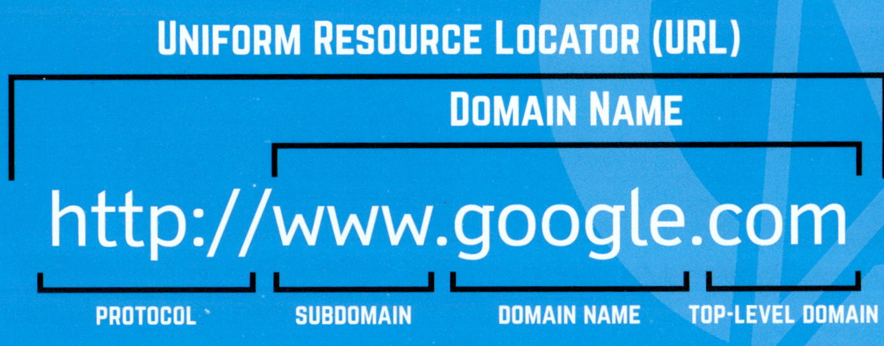

Mega Pixel
Madness
Delivered to your door
Everyday...
Fresh
Solution
Strategy
The World is Ours
GLOBAL
NETWORK
Home
Services
LOG IN
Username:
Password:
ENTER
Here!

CHAPTER 3

IT'S ALL IN THE PROTOCOLS

Computers use protocols to send information from one device to another. Transmission control protocol (TCP) breaks down the information into smaller pieces. Then Internet protocol (IP) tells those pieces where to go. These protocols are often referred to together as TCP/IP.

Computers use protocols to send and retrieve data or information.

When a person sends a file using the Internet, TCP breaks down the file into small chunks called **packets**. Packets are tiny. Each one contains fewer than 1,500 characters. TCP may break one file into thousands or millions of packets. Each packet has a header. The header has information about how to put the file back together.

Each packet also contains the sender's IP address and the receiver's IP address. IP uses this information to tell the packet where it needs to go. Then routers help the packet get to its destination. Routers tell the packet how to reach the receiver's

An e-mail message containing 3,500 bits of data might be split up into four packets.

IP address. They find the most efficient path for each packet.

Routers often work together to send a packet to its destination. The Internet is made up of many interconnected devices and wires. Sometimes one of them is busy or broken.

Computers use protocols to load and view websites.

Routers keep track of all the different ways they could send each packet to its destination. That way, if one of the devices or wires is busy or broken, routers can find a way to send the packets around the problem.

When the packets get to their destination, TCP checks to make sure that all the packets from the file have arrived. If any packets are missing, TCP sends a message back to the original computer. It asks the computer to resend the packets. Once all the packets reach their destination, TCP uses the information in the packet headers to put the file back together.

CRITICAL THINKING

Why is it important for TCP/IP to check that all of the packets arrive at their destination?

HTTP AND HTML

The World Wide Web is made up of many web pages. For a person to visit a web page, his or her computer must ask another computer for information. A protocol known as hypertext transfer protocol (HTTP) makes this possible.

HTTP is the set of rules that browsers and servers follow when asking for and receiving web documents. When a person types a URL into a web browser, the browser sends a message to the web server. This message is called a GET request. It asks the server for a web page.

The server sends the hypertext markup language (HTML) code for the web page to the web browser. HTML is the language that describes what web pages look like. HTML tags tell the browser how to display text. They also tell it where to put the graphics and videos. Each image or video on a web page has a separate HTTP GET

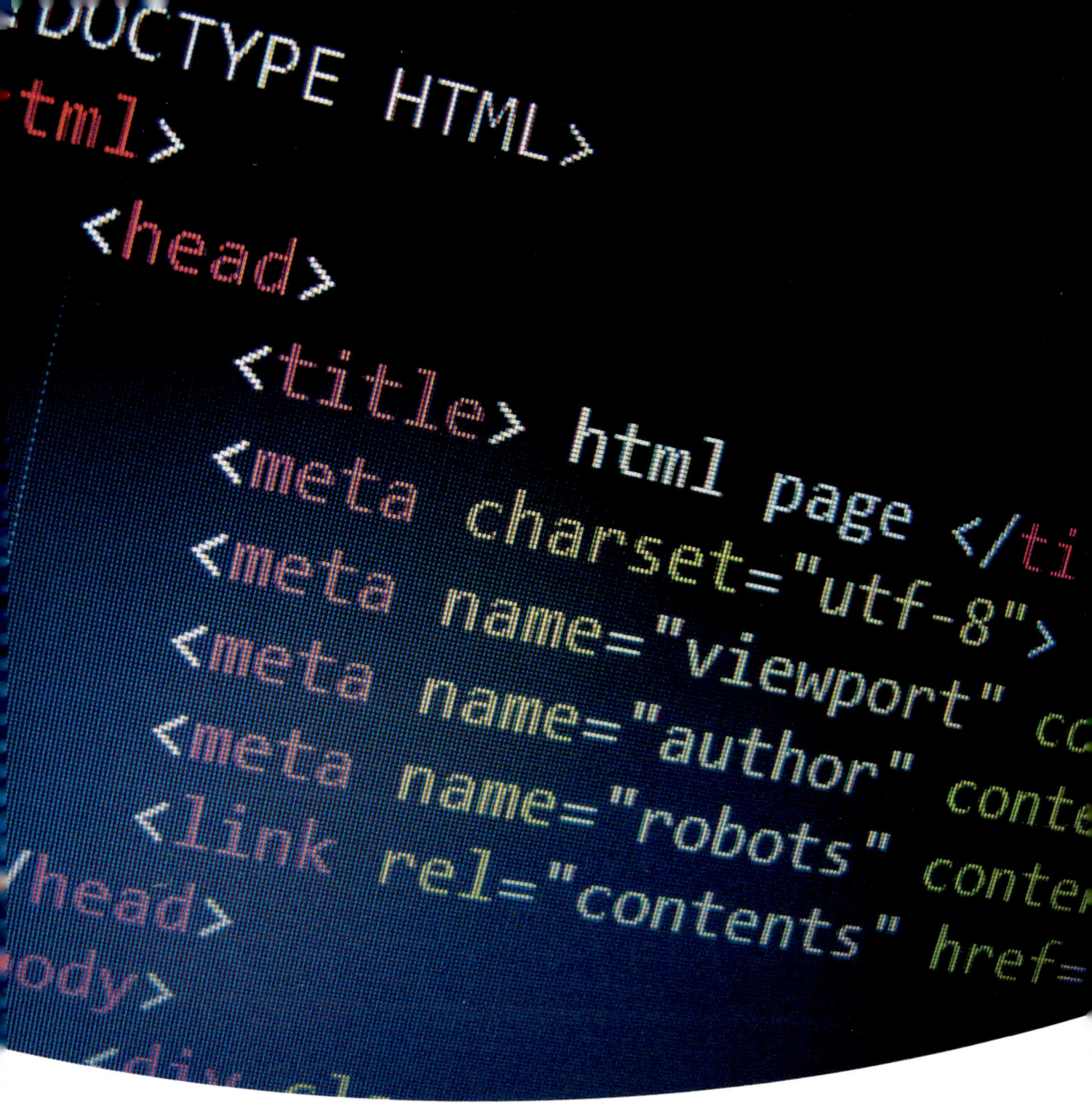

HTML code tells a browser how a web page should look.

request. This is why a page with a lot of photos or videos may load slowly.

CHAPTER 4

THE INTERNET OF THINGS

Today, computers are no longer the only way people connect to the Internet. Many people use devices such as smartphones or tablets to connect to the Internet on the go. Plus, a growing number of devices are part of the Internet of Things (IoT). Each device on the IoT can collect and transmit data.

Tablet users can stream videos, play online games, visit websites, and more.

A tablet can control the smart appliances in a home.

The IoT includes computers, sensors, and smart devices. Smart devices can be cars, televisions, and even appliances. Many are used in homes. These devices can control things such as thermostats, lights, or security systems. Wearable devices can track users' activity or sleep.

Some smart devices also analyze data. They may even make decisions. For example, the sensors in a car might be connected to a smart road system.

CRITICAL THINKING

Can you think of other household devices that might become part of the Internet of Things?

The system would use computers to monitor road conditions. It would look for accidents or traffic jams. It could also detect construction or bad weather. The system could reroute the car to avoid these things.

The IoT has potential applications in many other areas. Scientists might use the IoT to monitor air or water quality. Cities could use sensors to detect structural problems in bridges and roads. Doctors could use wearable devices to monitor patients at home. Sensors could detect a dangerous condition. They could then notify the doctor or call 911.

People continue to invent new uses for the IoT. The future is full of possibilities.

SMART DEVICES

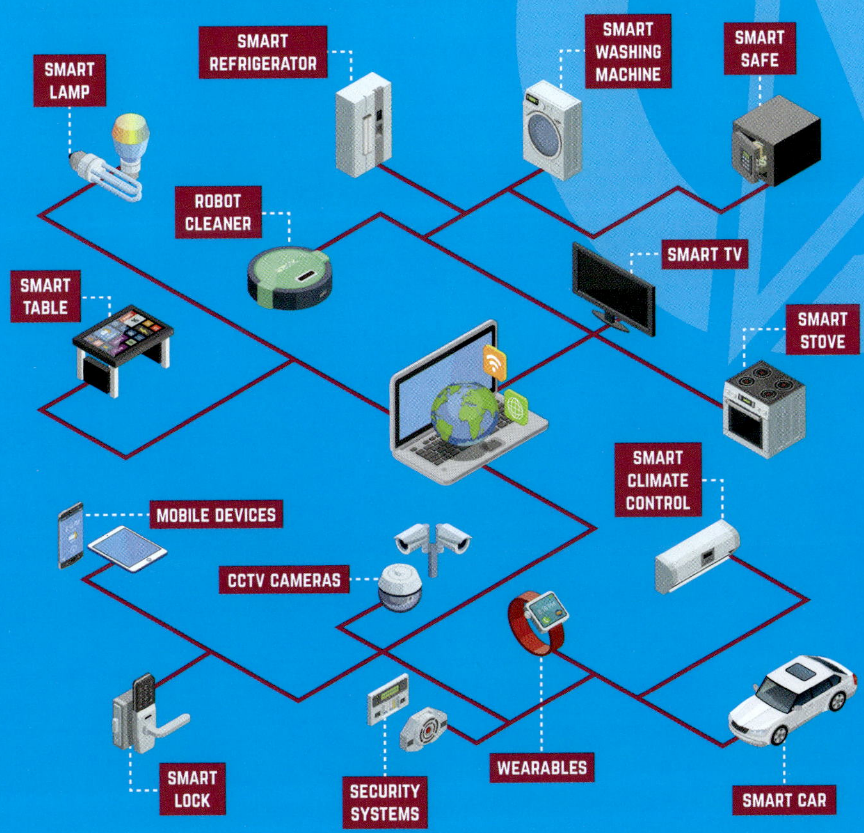

FOCUS ON

THE INTERNET

Write your answers on a separate piece of paper.

1. Write an e-mail to a friend explaining what you learned about how the Internet was invented.
2. Do you think linking together devices on the Internet of Things is a good idea? Why or why not?
3. Which protocol tells packets of information where to go?
    - **A.** transmission control protocol (TCP)
    - **B.** Internet protocol (IP)
    - **C.** hypertext transfer protocol (HTTP)
4. What might a router do if part of the Internet between the sender's IP address and the receiver's IP address is very busy?
    - **A.** It would find a faster route that sends the packets around the busy area.
    - **B.** It would delete the packets.
    - **C.** It would change the IP addresses in the packets' headers.

Answer key on page 32.

GLOSSARY

hypertext
Text or graphics a user can click on to get information from a document or go from one document to another.

packets
Amounts of information sent as single units from one computer to another.

protocol
A set of rules that computers use to communicate.

router
A device that sends information from one place to another.

servers
Computers that make data or programs available to other computers.

web browsers
Software applications that allow users to see and use websites.

web page
The information at a unique URL on the World Wide Web.

World Wide Web
A system of interconnected documents on the Internet that are identified by URLs and accessed using hypertext.

TO LEARN MORE

BOOKS

Hand, Carol. *How the Internet Changed History.* Minneapolis: Abdo Publishing, 2015.

Henzel, Cynthia Kennedy. *Inventing the Internet.* Mankato, MN: The Child's World, 2016.

Smibert, Angie. *12 Great Moments That Changed Internet History.* Mankato, MN: 12-Story Library, 2015.

NOTE TO EDUCATORS

Visit **www.focusreaders.com** to find lesson plans, activities, links, and other resources related to this title.

INDEX

Answer Key: 1. Answers will vary; **2.** Answers will vary; **3.** B; **4.** A